STEPHANIE JOHNSTONE, LCSW

TEACHING
SYSTEMIC
THINKING

TEACHING
SYSTEMIC
THINKING

by
David Campbell
Ros Draper
and
Clare Huffington

Systemic Thinking and Practice Series
Series Editors:
David Campbell and Ros Draper

KARNAC BOOKS
London 1991 New York

First published in 1988 by DC Publishing

This edition first published in 1991 by H. Karnac (Books) Ltd.,
58 Gloucester Road, London SW7 4QY

Distributed in the U.S.A. by
Brunner/Mazel, Inc
19, Union Square West,
New York, NY 10003

ISBN 1 85575 015 5

Printed in Great Britain by BPCC Wheatons Ltd, Exeter

Contents

Teaching Systemic Thinking

Dr David Campbell, MA, PhD, Principal Clinical Psychologist, Child and Family Department, Tavistock Clinic; Teacher and Supervisor, Institute of Family Therapy (London); Course Convenor, MSc in Family Therapy, Brunel University and Tavistock Clinic Joint Course.

Ros Draper, AAPSW Senior Social Worker, Organizing Tutor and Teacher, Child and Family Department, Tavistock Clinic; Teacher, Brunel University and Institute of Family Therapy (London); Consultant, Family Consultancy Service, Petersfield, Hampshire; Supervisor, Petersfield Counselling Service, Petersfield.

Clare Huffington, MSc, Cert Ed, ABPsS Principal Clinical Psychologist, Child and Family Department, Tavistock Clinic; Freelance Consultant to organizations.

Introduction

People kept asking us: *"Can you tell me how to do some more exercises on circular questioning?"*

So we began to think about writing a booklet like this. We decided to do so for two reasons. Firstly to share more exercises with people to help them, for example, become more confident interviewers because they know more about circular questioning. But secondly, to put the question of skills development into a wider context. There are many exercises people can practise in order to become more comfortable with systemic thinking and develop their systemic mind; and we have created many such exercises on our workshops and courses which we wanted to share.

We wanted to communicate some of the fun and excitement we have found in trying to teach systemic thinking in various teaching situations. For example, if a reader were to look at a hypothesizing or circular questioning exercise and ask us, for example, how to conduct it with a large group or a small group or mixed groups of professionals, we should *not* be able *not* to ask him/her questions about the specific context in which he/she was to teach and wanted to use the exercise. In order to know if it would be useful, we would want to know about the groups he/she was teaching and develop a hypothesis about why they want to learn something at this point in time. Then we might be able to develop ideas on the most helpful way of teaching them to ask circular questions; whether the circular questioning exercise should concern the participant's presence in the workshop, the requirements of their agency, the agency's relationship to family therapy or some other important area.

Interacting with students and trainees in particular ways, so as to create contexts in which systemic thinking can be developed for both teacher and trainee, has challenged us to develop our thinking further.

The booklet has evolved into various sections. We hope that it will be used as a resource by the readers. It can be thought of as an intervention to stimulate the reader's thinking and their own approach to teaching. We think that people learn in relation to a particular context. The meaning and impact of exercises derive entirely from the contexts in which they were developed and it is impossible here to fully convey the contexts of each of these exercises. However, the booklet may be a useful stimulus to people working in other contexts and we assume that the exercises given here would have to be modified and re-worked for people to use in their own settings.

This booklet may seem to generate a 'be spontaneous' paradox, since we are suggesting that teachers may find some of these ideas or exercises helpful, while also advocating that each teacher design his or her own exercises according to the feedback of the moment. But we know that the way people learn and develop their thinking best is by looking for feedback that challenges them. So we start looking at every new teaching situation by asking, "*What kind of challenge does this present to us?*", not, "*How can we teach them something we have taught before, and which they may therefore be expecting?*" We start by assuming that it is likely to be difficult to get new information into the system (learning is change), and we ask ourselves what we need to notice so as to be able to achieve this and create the feedback which will promote learning.

We have sometimes been asked about the relationship between our work and that of the Milan Team. Our job as teachers is to try to engage with a group and co-evolve in our learning. We do this with all the ideas, references and conversations we have ever had, tucked away in some semi-conscious reservoir. The extent to which we are connected to the Milan approach is a different issue from the one about teaching systemic thinking. We have had some ideas by ourselves and some might have come from an idea Cecchin told us about in 1982, or a conversation or supervision with Boscolo in 1984.

In some teaching settings it might enhance the learning process to look at the strong connection between us and the Milan team and then to Boscolo and Cecchin. Since the Milan team split up, we have had less interaction with them. We have taken their basic ideas and have developed our own vocabulary and style. For the purposes of recognition in the family therapy community, it may be helpful to refer to ourselves in connection with the Milan Approach, but, at a certain point, it ceases to be helpful to ask whether we are doing exactly what others are doing. When we are teaching, the aim is not to cite references, but to engage people with ideas. We are generally in the same ball park as the Milan Team, but beyond that, we do not see it as particularly helpful to trace our roots.

We would like to acknowledge our indebtedness to our colleague at the Tavistock Clinic, Dr Caroline Lindsey; to Margaret Robinson of the Family Consultancy Service in Hampshire; and to our trainees at the Tavistock, the Institute of Family Therapy and elsewhere in London, in Hampshire and overseas. They have participated with us in the interaction which has allowed us to develop this approach to teaching and training.

Part 1

Views on the Teaching and Learning Process

1. IMPORTANT PRINCIPLES

(a) The creation of a co-evolving system
The basis of teaching for us is the creation of a co-evolving system between the teachers and the participants. The co-evolutionary process provides the setting in which learning happens, but it also *is* the learning; it consists of the exchange between participants and observers and is about all of us being able to observe, in some way, that exchange. In creating a co-evolving system, we are aiming to create a context in which the participants are learning and we are learning. They are learning about systemic thinking and family therapy, and we are learning about teaching systemic thinking and family therapy.

We place great emphasis on the way we get feedback from participants about what they want right from the start of a teaching event, and this governs the way we spend the first day. It is important for us to let ourselves respond and be organized by what the group needs to develop, and not to teach from a script. We watch to see, for example, the differences and similarities among them relative to where they are in their learning. We try to get a sense of whether they are at Stage 1 or Stage 5 in that process, and what kind of blocks they might have that prevent them from moving on to the next stage. We speculate about that as we listen to their first bits of feedback; usually, for example, their expectations of the teaching event.

From their questions we gain a sense of whether people are new to systemic thinking or whether they have been struggling with it for some time. If people are at a basic level, they may be asking questions about theoretical issues such as positive connotation or neutrality. They may ask, for example, *"How can you be neutral if you really care about people?"*, or *"How can you work neutrally with life and death issues like child abuse and alcoholism?"* This would lead us in the direction of trying to do some exercises which would enable them to practise interviewing each other with a neutral stance.

If people are struggling with developing skills as therapists, they might be asking, "How do you create a hypothesis?" or "How do you test the hypothesis using feedback from the family?" We might then go forward designing exercises using role-play families to practise creating and testing out hypotheses using circular questioning.

Sometimes people have got issues like neutrality and basic skills under their belts, but have problems getting feedback from their own agencies about their position. For example, they might ask, "How can you work systemically when you have a statutory responsibility?" or "How can I take something back to my team?"! We might then go in the direction of exercises to get people to think about who in the agency might want them to be on the course and who might find that a threat.

In response to the questions the participants ask, the teachers continue to ask *themselves* questions in this action–reaction loop which constitutes the co-evolutional process. We are constantly asking ourselves where the participants are in relation to the ideas which have been generated; and this will take us on to the next stage of the teaching and learning process.

We will, for example, be looking for signs that the group is under too little or too much pressure. If too much time is given for the exercises, or too much time is devoted to explaining the instructions, people get bored. They may be so comfortable that there is no tension between their old ideas and the new ones, and therefore learning will not take place. On the other hand, if inadequate time is given or inadequate explanation, people may not have taken on enough of the experience for it to be useful to them outside the course. There may be too much tension for any accommodation to take place and the new ideas may be rejected.

A balance must be struck between didactic teaching and experiential teaching. We have sometimes made mistakes in the past about not offering enough didactic teaching, so that the group feels starved of the new ideas which create necessary tension for learning to take place.

(b) Attention to the group process

In placing great emphasis on the co-evolving system, one of the aims of the first day of teaching is to attend to the group process and to maintain this attention throughout a teaching event. This entails addressing the group process in order that people can feel connected to what is going on and to the other people. We often do specific pieces of work on this; for example we might ask, "How does X's comment affect what *you* think about this issue in your own agency?"

The nature of the teaching context will significantly affect the extent to which the group process can be developed. For example, in one or two day workshops, we access the group process less and we treat the participants more as individuals attached to agencies. At the other end of the scale, on year-long seminars or a training, there are more possibilities for creating a co-evolving system in which the group process becomes facilitative of change. The spaces between sessions and the passage of time while on the course create the opportunity for a wider-ranging group process in which a greater variety of experience is used for learning, particularly feedback from the participants' own agencies. There is time for participants to describe their own work settings, to listen to others' descriptions and compare their experiences. Sometimes projects are organized and people meet each other in their own agencies outside the course.

(c) Becoming observers of the learning process

Learning involves an oscillating dynamism between experience and observation of that experience. People are always asked to jump from the participating to the observing level. It is implicit in this approach that you cannot *not* learn and you are learning all the time. Part of the job of teachers is to enable the participants to see themselves as learning all the time, and not only when they think they are being taught.

In moving back and forth between experience and observation of that experience, the participants are also oscillating between linear and systemic views and between content and process issues. It is important to acknowledge that participants have linear views, and that they see themselves as part of a cause-and-effect context. They also often have to be preoccupied in their agencies with collecting data about families, for example, the circumstances of sex abuse. It is, however, in the movement between these linear views and content issues and a wider systemic perspective, together with the observation of this movement, that a third new context can be created. This we call experiencing a co-evolving reality.

(d) Moving between contexts

Participants learn by having the experience of being systemic thinkers, but also by having many different experiences. They might move from interviewing a role-play family to interviewing a colleague about a work setting to being a family member to listening to a lecture, but are always being asked to think systemically. What happens in one context meets and reverberates with what happens in another, so as to create a third context in which the first two are joined in a recursive relationship, and this breaks new ground in the participants' thinking.

If people are confused or put into an unpredictable context, but there are also enough elements of familiar territory or ideas, there will be some interplay between the new confusing ideas and the old ones to create some kind of hybrid or amalgam of the two. Confusion represents the cognitive challenge to the participants' old map of how things are. This struggle to create new ideas often leaves course participants exhausted at the end of the day.

We try to teach in a way that is congruent with a therapy model by creating a context in which people can make new connections. The teachers, like therapists, remain in charge of the pace and flow of learning. They ultimately have to decide, "Is it better to have a coffee break and change the context? Or is it better to keep pushing on and following through on these points until participants are almost clear?" The teachers have to be vigorous, active and rather bossy in creating a structure within which people have the freedom to explore their thinking at their own pace.

(e) Playfulness and humour

Playfulness and humour are important aspects of the co-evolving process in that they do two things. Firstly, they create an environment in which people feel safe by being acknowledged and understood in the difficulties they are facing in their work – a feeling of all being in the same boat. Secondly, they work paradoxically to shift the context. For example, if people were talking about their problems in doing exercises on the course and someone were to say, "You think this is bad but it'll be worse tomorrow!", this changes the context into one in which people are no longer doing the worst they have ever done, so maybe they can do it after all!

(f) Difference and connectedness

As a teacher, it is important to push people back and forth between the awareness of difference and the awareness of connectedness. We try to do this in many ways. We might, for example, ask a pair to discuss the main differences between the way they see a family and then ask them to stop and consider the connection between the two different views.

Also, we have found that if you push people, in discussion, toward extremes and opposites in their thinking, they will resolve the opposites through their own thinking and conversation. If we can enable people to be aware of this process, we can enable them to appreciate this aspect of systemic thinking.

(g) The power of a question

We believe in asking questions and do it throughout our teaching. They are interventions. They trigger an internal process whereby the 'learner' rearranges his/her own thoughts to incorporate the question and create a new ecology. But a question seems more neutral and can be rejected, reworded, etc., to suit the needs of the learner.

As teachers, our questions, like our questions as therapists, challenge the learner to declare him/herself and define his/her relationship to new ideas. Hypothetical future questions and reflective questions are particularly useful in a teaching context.

2

What Teaching Does for the Teachers

The teaching that really works in getting *teachers* engaged with systemic thinking is the teaching that gives people the experience of participating in a co-evolving system. As teachers, we are actively involved in finding ways of responding to the participants' ideas. If they can observe the teachers being influenced by their feedback and taking this feedback to a higher level of organization in which the teacher's comments to them have included their feedback, then participants see the systemic process in action. This is what is exciting for everybody.

The working partnership between us (D.C. and R.D.) as teachers can also be seen as a co-evolving process from which the participants might learn. While there are differences in style which influence the way we teach, we are affected by and interested in what each other has to say. This is the reason we have worked together for such a long time.

Our roles are not fixed in that, although D.C. often leads the theoretical discussion and R.D. begins an interview, these roles might be reversed to generate some new ideas for both of us. During a workshop we tend to alternate taking charge of a discussion and exercises, in order to create differences for the participants and give each other the chance to step back, rest and observe the process of teaching and learning.

We tend to engage different kinds of people in different ways. D.C. engages certain kinds of people better than R.D., and vice versa. We have about the same amounts of pride and self-effacing behaviour. Neither will step too far back into the shadows, and neither wants to dominate. One might say, "I want to get my oar in, I haven't been doing much," and the other might say, "I'll step back, I've had my oar in too long." This is a good bit of chemistry that enables us to teach well.

We are each interested in the effect feedback from the group has on one another, and learn from the way each of us connects similarly or differently with a piece of information from one group; and we are each interested in what the other says and does. Showing that interest allows course participants to experience, in another way, being part of a co-evolving process and system.

3

Teaching Contexts

We have been teaching family therapy for many years in many different contexts. These contexts have been important in affecting the way we teach by presenting certain limitations and possibilities. These provide the basis for making a hypothesis about how best the participants will be engaged in new ideas. We are always asking ourselves what is the minimum intervention that will produce the maximum change? The experiences described in this paper are taken from four important teaching contexts.

(a) One- or two-day workshops
These can involve up to 30 participants, or even more, depending on the demand. The aim is to challenge people's way of thinking and to give them an introduction or overview of the main theoretical ideas and techniques. One small goal is to make a punctuation in people's thinking rather than expect them to have a co-evolutionary experience, since the time constraint and group size means there is less opportunity for feedback and interaction of ideas.

Our main task is to keep the participants engaged in the events of the day. We have to work hard to generalize from what the participants say to create a conceptual framework which fits their goals and allows us to cover the material planned for the day. If the group is smaller or we have more time, it is more possible to let things evolve. In a group of 30, however, we would still attempt to give the participants some experience of working in a smaller unit, so some of the exercises would involve working in small groups of 3 or 4.

In some ways, we would see the one- or two-day workshops as an introductory exercise themselves. It may be less exciting for the teachers, but maybe out of this, 10% will get interested in the ideas and come back another time.

(b) Five-day intensive workshops
These can involve 12 to 16 participants. The aim is to create a co-evolving system in which the group process can become facilitative. There is more time for the participants to develop ideas and connections between them, as well as listen to each other, share experiences and practise skills. It is more possible for each individual to express his/her goals and for these to receive attention and become connected to the group process. The effect of not returning to their own agencies throughout the course is that the group process becomes much more intense. Consequently we spend time at the end of the course helping the participants to leave the course and get re-engaged with the problems in their own agencies.

(c) One-year weekly or fortnightly seminars
These can involve about 12 to 16 participants, sometimes working in groups of 3 or 4, but often as a large group since they come to know one another very well during the year. The aim is to create a co-evolving system including more of the participants' own agency systems. The basic unit of interaction is thus the worker and his/her agency. It is possible in a course over a longer period with gaps between sessions to obtain feedback about how participants are taking new ideas back to their agencies, the effect on their colleagues and any problems they are facing as a result. These experiences will interact with the experiences of the other participants to create a much wider ranging, more complex and differentiated group process. The session time of 2.5 hours seems to create the right amount of space to allow participants to really develop their ideas and learn rapidly.

(d) One-year training and supervision groups

We teach on a one-year course which involves live supervision as well as theoretical and skills development. The course contains up to 9 people placed in groups of 3 or 4 to make therapy teams. The course is for those who want to see themselves develop more fully as clinicians and systemic thinkers.

Usually, they are already working with the systemic approach but want the space to practise and refine their work. We engage people about where they think they want to get to in their development. Our goal is to create a process in which they can pace their own development and in particular take more risks in their thinking and practice with families.

The basic unit of interaction shifts from worker and agency to therapist and family. Much of the time is spent observing the interaction between family and therapist and commenting upon it, doing exercises and reading, doing a tape review of it and so on, in order to help the therapist engage and work with the family differently.

We have to think carefully about our role as supervisors in the relationship between the therapist, family and supervisor/team and, because it is a training and live families are involved, professional issues, such as clinical responsibility, are covered.

Part II

Components of Teaching

1. THEORETICAL INPUT

We tend to teach theory in several ways. We have found it is
very effective to link a theoretical discussion to an exercise. For
example, an exercise about formulating the family as a system
can be followed by a discussion during which we might elabor-
ate the concept of the interconnectedness of meaning and
behaviour by referring to the experiences which the participants
had during the exercise. This is a powerful method of conveying
ideas.

We also like to have periods of general discussion in the large
group, and from the questions raised, one of us might go to the
"blackboard" to make a diagram, or outline some points which
help to clarify a theoretical point. During each of our workshops
we would inevitably present the theoretical framework which
underpins our own thinking and the concepts presented during
the workshop. This presentation usually takes about an hour, as
it is accompanied by diagrams and key words and phrases
whenever possible.

The content of the the theoretical framework is slightly

different each time we present because we are inevitably influenced by the most recent discussion or case we have taken part in and also because changing the approach keeps us fresh and interested in our own presentation. There is nothing worse for a teacher than to become bored by the sound of his or her own voice.

However, there are some theoretical concepts we find very helpful for participants grappling to develop their own systemic thinking.

1.   A *system* is any unit structured on feedback. We emphasize the importance of creating and observing feedback processes in every situation which requires systemic thinking.

2.   Feedback over time becomes identified as *pattern*.

3.   The identification of the pattern introduces the concept of the *observer* of the pattern. No pattern exists without someone on the scene who punctuates events in such a way that they are seen as a pattern (*see* Maturana, 1978).

4.   Pattern creates its own *context*, and it is only through context that events or behaviours acquire meaning.

5.   Meaning and behaviour have a *recursive* or *circular relationship*. We voluntarily behave as we do because we have certain beliefs about the context we are in, and our beliefs are supported or challenged by the feedback from our behaviour.

6.   Meanings which are attributed to behaviour can be arranged in a *hierarchical structure*. Some meanings come from more inclusive and more abstract levels such as religion and culture, whereas other meanings come from lower order, more specific levels such as dyadic relationships (*see* Cronen and Pearce, 1985).

7.   Symptomatic behaviour arises from an individual's attempt to create a new relationship or a new pattern of feedback in response to perceived changes going on within or around him.

8. When this individual behaviour is observed and responded to by members of an interconnected system, the *feedback loop* acquires meaning from a larger context than originally constructed by the individual. In this way a problem is only a problem if it is labelled as such by some observer (or observing group).

9. Concepts such as 'problem', 'badness', 'strangeness' describe an interactive process between the 'observer' and the 'observed'. And as these people interact they become a system and their behaviour has meaning for the larger system around them.

10. What's important about problems is understanding the meaning which underlies the relationship created between the *'problem bearer'*, and the consequences for the wider system of seeing things that way.

11. We assume that families approach therapists because they feel something important is changing. The change frightens some family members, and they want the therapist to change the way things are changing.

12. The aim of therapy is to create a context in which the family and individuals can think differently about the problem behaviour.

13. The therapist does this by introducing differences to the way people think by listening carefully to understand their beliefs, and then posing questions which subtly shift those beliefs or behaviours into new contexts.

14. There are many interviewing techniques, such as circular questioning, which are invaluable tools in this process; however, they will be discussed in the next paper in the series.

15. Therapists get stuck when they have only a partial view of the system – if they lose sight of the family's wish to change or remain the same. For this reason we present many ideas about the family's struggle to achieve a balance

between stability and change.

16. The referring person, the family members and the therapist and his/her team are all a part of a *'problem-determined system'* (*see* Anderson *et al.*, 1987) which assumes the same features of interconnectedness and balance between stability and change which are characteristic of any application of systems thinking.

17. Finally, the view which a therapist and team take of the family will be affected by the context in which the therapist finds him or herself. For example, in some contexts the therapist must act directly to protect children; in other contexts the therapist can leave the responsibility for change with the family.

2

Group Discussion

We see discussion as a means whereby the system interacts and creates new information. It is also an expression of the connectedness in the group over time. For the teachers, managing a discussion means managing the balance between the needs of the group and the needs of individuals. The same question from one person has a different meaning when asked by somebody else in the group who has a different history. We ask ourselves, "What does this question represent for this person? What has precipitated this question in this person's struggles in their own work?" We try to answer in a way that allows them to reflect back on that context. If the question seems disconnected from the systemic process and is asked in a didactic way, we might be more cheeky and challenging: "What difference would it make to your thinking if we answered this question?"

We listen to see how people have been affected by our feedback to them. People start asking questions based on premises presented by the teachers. Sometimes people seem not to have been part of the group process and ask questions based on the premise they came with.

When this happens, such a question will often be answered by another question asking them to think about the system of relationships or ideas which generated that question in the first place.

In order for an answer to a question to be useful to particip-ants, the teachers need to get them to look at how they are learning. How will the answer contribute to the process of their learning?

3

Video Presentation and
Live Family Session

Video presentation creates a context in which people can match their expectations of what they see people do and don't do in family therapy. It allows people to become engaged through learning what is safe. They are able to put their own learning into that context by asking themselves what do they do that you don't, and so on.

A visual experience like this can be very powerful if the participants are asked questions in such a way that they place themselves in relation to the video material.

Questions
1. In a group, look for 3 ways in which verbal and non-verbal material confirms/disconfirms the hypothesis.

2. What is the interaction between the hypothesis and the feedback from the family that would lead you to be stuck as the therapist? Give 3 examples.

3. What contradictions are emerging from the questioning

in the belief system and behaviour of the family?

4.   What issues need to be addressed in an intervention?

It is not possible, in our experience, to remain engaged with video for longer than about 10 minutes.

Live families can be more engaging than video presentation in that participants feel galvanized by the riskiness of not knowing what is going to happen. In this context, people can get involved in creating a system around the therapy as it is going on. The kind of question we ask observers of a live family session would be: "In terms of the development of your epistemology or technique, what questions would you like to have answered in the family session today?"

A great deal of attention is paid to how the participants observe and they will have questions to answer, hypotheses to watch for, and things to look for.

READING AND WRITING – HOMEWORK – TAKING NOTES

We think of these next three chapters as interventions, in that they involve an explicit attempt to challenge the participant's ecology of ideas.

4

Reading and Writing

(A) READING

Our general approach to reading is to ask people how they have been challenged by what they have read. In this respect, it is congruent with the feedback process, modelling the theory of the relationship between beliefs and behaviour. In order for behaviour to change, beliefs must be challenged, leading to the creation of a new context in which alternative behaviours are possible. We start by asking, "What difference has it made to people to read this paper or book?", "Which ideas does it threaten and which does it validate?" We are far more interested in the effect the paper has on the reader's thinking than in clarifying the meaning of the paper as intended by the author. We find that clarification questions arise out of the participants' attempts to answer the questions about what difference the paper has made. We then spend some time asking, for example, what Karl Tomm means when he is talking about 'reflexive questions', and whether he means this or that particular thing.

We organize the reading from the key references found at the end of this booklet. We have found the following references most helpful under each of these general headings:

1. Developing systemic thinking

Bateson, G. (1973) 'The cybernetics of "self": a theory of alcoholism', in *Steps to an Ecology of Mind*. London: Paladin, pp. 280–308.

Keeney, B. (1983) *Aesthetics of Change*. New York: Guildford Press.

Watzlawick, P. *et al.* (1968) *Pragmatics of Human Communication*. New York and London: W.W. Norton.

2. Differences among models of family therapy

Hoffman, L. (1981) *Foundations of Family Therapy*. New York: Basic Books.

Liddle, H.A. (1968) 'On the problem of eclecticism, a call for epistemological clarification and human scale theories.' *Family Process*, **21**, pp. 243–249.

MacKinnon, L. (1983) 'Contrasting strategic and Milan therapies.' *Family Process*, **22**, pp. 425–437.

3. The Milan approach: overview and basic concepts

Campbell, D. *et al.* (1983) *Working with the Milan Method: Twenty Questions*. London: London Institute of Family Therapy.

Palazzoli, M.S. *et al.* (1978) *Paradox and Counter Paradox*. New York and London: Aronson.

Palazzoli, M.S. *et al.* (1980) 'Hypothesizing – circularity – neutrality: three guidelines for the conductor of the session.' *Family Process*, **19**, pp. 3–12.

Palazzoli, M.S. *et al.* (1978) 'The problem of the referring person.' *Journal of Marital and Family Therapy*, **6**, pp. 3–9.

Penn, P. (1982) 'Circular questioning.' *Family Process*, **20**, pp. 267–280.

Tomm, K. (1984) 'One perspective on the Milan systemic approach: Part I, Overview of development, theory and practice.' *Journal of Marital and Family Therapy*, **10**, pp. 113–125.

Tomm, K. (1984) 'One perspective on the Milan systemic approach: Part II, Description of session format and interviewing style and intervention.' *Journal of Marital and Family Therapy*, **10**, pp. 253–271.

These are examples of questions we have put to various groups in relation to papers they have read to create the kind of discussion we have described as challenging and helpful:

1.   What was the most challenging and difficult idea?

2.   What was the idea which has become clearest?

3.   What ideas do e.g., the Mendez *et al.* paper 'The bringing forth of pathology' and, e.g., the Tomm papers have in common?

4.   Which ideas came most into focus?

5.   Which ideas did you most have to grapple with?

6.   Which of those would you put on the agenda for future discussion?

7.   Which ideas do you find most and least helpful?

8.   How do the key premises behind the paper affect practice in your agency?

9.   How does this paper affect the way you generate hypotheses?

10.   What is the difference between the Milan approach to hypothesis-making and general formulations about families?

11.   What do you find most difficult and most valuable about neutrality?

12.   Which of the ideas you have learned about today are you going to incorporate in your work next week?

13.   Are any of the ideas applicable to a case you are currently working with or stuck with? Which ones and how?

(B) WRITING

Writing is an extremely useful way for people to clarify their own thoughts, regardless of whether they feel they can write or have any experience of writing. We usually stipulate that they should write no more than a page, so that it looks like a manageable task and so that it forces them to distil their own ideas succinctly. We often ask people to write in conjunction with reading. Some examples follow.

Example 1
On: Penn, P. (1985) 'Feed forward: future questions, future maps.' *Family Process*, **24**, pp. 299–310.

and Tomm, K. (1985) 'Circular interviewing: a multifaceted clinical tool.' in Campbell, D. and Draper, R. (Eds.), *Applications of Systemic Family Therapy: The Milan Approach.* London: Grune and Stratton.

Write an essay on how to do circular questioning and give an example from your own clinical work on the course.

Example 2
On: Palazzoli, M.S. *et al.* (1980) 'Hypothesizing – circularity – neutrality.'

and Tomm, K. (1987) 'Interventive interviewing.' Parts I, II and III,

and Ugazio, V. (1985) 'Hypothesizing revisited' in Campbell, D. and Draper, R. (Eds.) *Applications of Systemic Family Therapy: The Milan Approach.*

1.   Write a page on what you are looking for in order to make

a hypothesis when observing a family for the first time and subsequently.

2.   Give an example from something you have seen on the course.

Example 3
On: Treacher, A. (1988) 'The Milan method: a preliminary critique.' *Journal of Family Therapy*, **10**, 1, pp. 1–8.
Write an outline response to the above article.

In some of our courses, we include the requirement of a written position paper at the end of a term or of the course. A position paper is a paper in which people are asked to clarify their own position in relation to the various important theoretical issues in family therapy, such as:

1.   What is the role of the therapist in family therapy?

2.   How do you explain the process of change?

3.   What is the function of the symptom?

4.   How does the system get organized?

5.   What causes people to change?

6.   What issues do you need to address to create a context for change?

Sometimes, we ask people to share their position papers with one another and make comments on the differences and connections between them.

5

Homework

We set homework questions throughout courses to begin the process of creating feedback in the back-home situation. These tend to be questions that address change more generally with the aim of creating ripples in a wider range of thinking and practice. They give course participants a chance to step back and evaluate what is happening to them during the time they are on the course. In answering such questions participants get a different perspective on the course from simply participating in it. At the same time, we are aware of the practical issues of fatigue and the fact that participants sometimes wish to forget the course for a while. We usually spend some time at the beginning of the next session using the homework as a focus for discussion.

Example 1
Write down the question that is most important for you to have answered at the moment. Then pass it on to someone else to answer overnight. This person is asked to write a response to bring to the course the next day. The written answers to the questions are shared in large groups or in foursomes if the group

is too large for each question to be shared around.

Example 2
What is it about your relationship to us as course leaders that makes it more or less difficult to learn about the Milan approach?

Example 3
1.   What is the Milan approach and is it an ideology?

2.   What are the boundaries/limitations of systemic thinking?

3.   Where is systemic thinking in relation to systemic family therapy?

Example 4
What are some of the most important ideas/beliefs that you would have to give up if you were to move on with this way of working?

We have done workshops with longer time gaps between one workshop and another and have given people an assignment to write something after the first workshop. For example:

1.   Predict what you will be doing differently in your work as a result of this seminar.

2.   How will you behave differently in your own agency as a result of thinking about your agency in a systemic way?

On the occasion of the second workshop, participants could look at the papers again and see whether they were able to behave differently.

6

Taking Notes

We are always trying to take feedback to another level. We tend to ask people to structure their feedback to exercises and other experiences on courses in order that people monitor their own learning. Some examples follow.

(a) Recording family therapy sessions
We ask trainees, who are acting as team members, to take notes as they are observing family therapy sessions. In the context of a supervision group, the recording can take the form of verbatim notes often linked to annotation of the video tape, recording the place in the video where a particular question was asked or a significant piece of interaction observed. This is also useful for the therapist when he/she is reviewing the tape. Sessions can also be recorded in terms of themes emerging like competition, mourning or loyalty; how the hypothesis is developed; how the family respond to certain questions; the supervisor's comments; contradictions between beliefs and between beliefs and behaviour; reflexive questioning and responses to these; and so on.

(b) Writing up family therapy sessions
We ask trainees to write brief notes on each family therapy

session covering the following topics:

1.   Summary of the referral process (for first session).

2.   Pre-session discussion – main points.

3.   Initial hypothesis.

4.   Main themes of session.

5.   Intervention – verbatim.

6.   Feedback from intervention – verbatim, plus non-verbal behaviour.

7.   Date of next appointment.

8.   Ideas for next hypothesis.

We find it particularly useful if people manage to jot down some ideas from the post-session discussion for the next hypothesis. It means that they are placing themselves in the process of evolving ideas with the family.

(c) Written feedback on courses
An example of this is where trainees were asked to write down after each session:

1.   One idea that was useful.

2.   One idea that was puzzling or difficult.

3.   What the supervisor did today that made a difference to the way you think about therapy.

4.   Whether anything that was said today presented a challenge to you as a systemic thinker.

Observations were collected in a book or file for trainees to see at the end of term to observe their own and others' development and how their difficulties were dealt with.

7

Exercises

INTRODUCTION

Creating exercises is an essential part of the process of teaching systemic thinking. Primarily it allows us, as teachers, to respond to the feedback we get from course members and transform it into a structured event which allows the participants to push their learning on to the next stage.

The structure of the exercise enables the participant to experience specific conceptual features of systemic thinking (such as the role of the observer and the problem-determined system) through action. We believe that learning is more profound when it takes place in a context that combines thought and action. An exercise also creates the space for participants to reflect on their own experience, and they learn only what they are ready to learn. We expect each participant to 'need' different experiences to advance their learning and we find the use of exercises allows participants to have many different experiences while relating to a common theme which has emerged from the group process during the workshop.

We have grouped the exercises into sections according to the area of systemic thinking or practice for which the exercise is designed. They are described in roughly sequential order. Each one is followed (or preceded) by comments about the important features of the exercise, and the effect it appears to have on the participants.

We recognize that the power of an exercise arises from the way the exercise is created from the feedback of the group, its co-evolutionary potential; and that taken out of the context in which they are used, the exercises may lose their meaning. But nevertheless, we think our experiences may be helpful or interesting to others as they develop their own approaches to teaching systemic thinking.

(A) 'EXPECTATION' EXERCISES

Exercise 1

1. The participants are asked to join in pairs and one person asks the other circular questions about what he or she wants to achieve between now and the end of the course. He/she tries to understand what makes these things important to the other person (a) professionally and (b) personally.

2. After about 10 minutes, the interviewer pauses to make a hypothesis based on the information given.

3. The interviewer then continues asking questions around the hypothesis for another 10 minutes.

4. Following this, the interviewer stops to make a formulation about the meaning of these expectations. This is then shared with the interviewee, who is invited to give some feedback.

5. The same exercise is repeated with each of the partners changing places. We ask participants to write down their formulations and the feedback if we plan to refer to this towards the end of a course.

Discussion
This exercise is useful in enabling participants to declare their expectations and think of them being connected to other important contexts. It also introduces them to the practice of hypothesizing, interviewing and formulating in a way that 'breaks the ice' and allows pairs to get to know each other.

Exercise 2
1.   Each participant is asked to think individually about:
    (a)   What he/she wants to get from the course;
    (b)   Three or four people who will be most affected by his/her being on the course.

2.   Then each person is asked to discuss with another person sitting near them: *What will happen to these relationships –*
    (a)   If you get what you want from the course?
    (b)   If you do not get what you want from the course?

Discussion
This exercise connects each person's participation on the course with the wider system of relationships in back-home agencies. It is a powerful way to introduce this type of thinking and it is useful for people who are not yet familiar with hypothesizing and circular questioning.

Exercise 3

1. In pairs, participants are asked to introduce themselves to each other and find out the other's expectations of the course.

2. In pairs, they are asked to reflect on how what they have learned about their partner will affect his/her relationship with the course and to his/her learning. This takes about 10 minutes.

3. Each person is then asked to introduce his/her partner to the whole group, including his/her expectations.

4. We sometimes take this a bit further by asking the participants to formulate questions they would like to raise in the whole group and to think about how the questions relate to their expectations of the course.

Discussion

This exercise is useful in a smaller sized group (8–20) in which the group leader would like to have the participants meet and hear about other members in the group and it requires no previous exposure to specific interviewing techniques.

Exercise 4
During courses lasting several days, we have frequently begun by placing the participants in groups of four to discuss expectations and keeping them in these groups throughout the day to practise technique and do role play. Then, at the end of the day, we ask the group members to reflect on their experience of being part of that group system by asking them to discuss some or all of the following questions:

1. What was the effect on your individual expectations of the course of being in a group of four?

2. What was the greatest area of conflict between what you wanted as individuals and what you wanted as a group?

3. Which of the four of you learned most in the course of being in the group? How would you understand that?

4. Who do you think found it most difficult to approach their expectations as a result of being in the group?

5. If your group were to continue tomorrow, would it need to change to meet the needs of individuals in the group? How?

Discussion
The group discussions generate a great deal of feedback and new ideas for each member. We find people are quickly involved in the course and they begin to take responsibility for their own learning as a member of the group. They also begin to observe themselves as part of the learning context.

(B) 'MAKING A SYSTEM' EXERCISES

Exercise 5 – Experiencing the family as a system

1. The participants in the group are asked to think to themselves about a role they would like to play in a family and how they might behave to maintain that role.

2. Then they are asked to get into groups of four and negotiate with the group to make some kind of family which incorporates everyone's roles. The discussion should be done sequentially and each person should preface their comments by saying, "If (the previous person) were to behave in that way I would want to behave in such-and-such a way." (Members are not 'in-role' but talking *about* their roles.) This should take about 5 minutes and the discussion should pass around the group 2 or 3 times.

3. Then one person in each group (randomly chosen) is asked to think about doing something different which would ensure they were able to get more of their needs met (in their role) in the newly constructed family groups.

4. The other group members then discuss, in sequence, how they would have to change *their* behaviour to accommodate to the first person's changed behaviour without relinquishing their own needs.

5. The groups now are asked to imagine the family group is splintering and they would each like to preserve the family if possible. Each person is asked to comment, in sequence, on how they could behave to unify the family without relinquishing their own needs (5 minutes).

6. Each group is asked to de-role themselves and share their experiences of each other. Finally the large group is reassembled and general points are gathered from the group.

Discussion
This exercise is a powerful way to allow people less familiar with family therapy to experience the 'systemic' qualities of family life. The sequential discussion is essential here because it allows each person to

change in response to the previous speaker and as this process con- inues, a systemic reality is called for in the group. There are many possible variations of tasks which can be set for the small groups, and this exercise leads very well into a more theoretical discussion about family systems.

Exercise 6

1.   The participants are asked to join in foursomes and one
      person asks the other three about any topic or themselves
      as a system. The three are asked to form a system as they
      go along by responding sequentially to the feedback from
      the group and the interviewer.

2.   After about 15 minutes, the interviewer pauses to make a
      hypothesis about the system.

3.   The interviewer then continues asking questions around
      the hypothesis for another 10 minutes.

4.   Feedback by both interviewer and the three interviewees is
      structured around each hypothesizing from their position
      in the system about the contradictory behaviour and areas
      of difficulty and conflict in the system.

Discussion
This exercise is a powerful tool for helping people appreciate the way in
which one person's behaviour organizes another's, and so on,
recursively.

(C) 'HYPOTHESIZING' EXERCISES

Exercise 7

1. The participants are asked to join in foursomes and to work together to make a hypothesis about a letter or referral.

2. If there is a large group, the hypotheses from all the groups may be recorded on the board and the group discuss them.

3. In foursomes again, each person formulates one or two questions based on the hypothesis, puts the question to the others and practises using the feedback to ask 3 or 4 more questions. To do this most efficiently, the questioner quickly assigns roles, such as 'You be mother, you be child', and then puts the question to whomever they choose. The selected family member replies, in role, which leads the questioner to ask several more questions based on that feedback.

4. As a variation, or addition, each person could articulate the hypothesis, then ask the question and then discuss how they process it before producing the next question.

5. The exercise is then discussed in the small and large groups.

Discussion
This exercise attempts to challenge the idea that every question has to be a 'good one'. Instead, we want to convey the notion that the most important feature of hypothesizing and circular questioning is learning to join and be aware of the feedback process. When the therapist is able to do this, questions will naturally arise; they don't have to be dredged up in some artificial or forced manner.

Exercise 8

1. Participants are asked to join in threesomes with an interviewer, interviewee and observer, the interviewee selecting a case for which he/she needs a hypothesis.

2. The interviewer interviews the interviewee about the case for about 10 minutes.

3. Then the interviewer and the observer discuss the case in front of the interviewee in order to develop several hypotheses about the case. They are particularly instructed to discard one or more of the hypotheses during their discussion.

4. The interviewee then becomes the observer of the process and is asked to comment on why certain hypotheses were discarded while others were retained.

5. Then either the small groups or the large group are asked to observe their own learning process by considering three questions:
    (a) What questions were raised for you about hypothesis-making?
    (b) What became clearer?
    (c) What problems are there for you now about hypothesis-making?

Discussion
The advantage of this exercise is that it allows the 'stuck' therapist to observe his/her case through the eyes of new, more objective observers; and in doing so, the therapist achieves more distance from the case. It also introduces the notion of discarding hypotheses, since we often feel therapists get stuck because they cannot 'let go' of ideas (rather than being unable to generate new ideas).

Exercise 9

1.   Participants are asked to join in foursomes with a therapist, observer, and two family members. They are asked to set up a role-play with the therapist interviewing the family to find out the problem and map the significant system. The two family members briefly create a problem and their own hypotheses about the meaning of the problem for the wider system.

2.   The therapist and the observer together make their own hypothesis.

3.   The therapist continues questioning, but after each question pauses to make the statements to the observer, "This makes me think X about a relationship or a belief" before asking the next question.

4.   During each pause, the therapist and the observer may revise the hypothesis on the basis of the response to the questions.

5.   After about 15 to 20 minutes, the foursomes are asked to stop and discuss the exercise. The therapist is asked to comment on his/her thinking before and after making statements about the relationship between belief and behaviour and how this affected the process of hypothesizing. The observer is asked to comment on the process of the interview; the family members on the way they were organized by specific questions.

Discussion
We often use exercises which explore interviewing technique by 'slowing down the action'. This enables participants to get a feel of the process of using feedback to alter their thinking about the family and to feel some confidence in the technique before they are exposed to the pressures of a family therapy interview. We find that the other part-icipants gain equally by observing the interviewer struggling to do this.

(D) 'INTERVIEWING' EXERCISES

Exercise 10

1.   In threesomes, each participant is asked to think about a problem he/she might have in working with families in his/her place of work.

2.   Each person describes the conflicts or contradictions he/she experiences in trying to deal with this problem.

3.   One person agrees to be interviewed by another and the third acts as observer.

4.   The interviewer (for about 10 minutes) should use circular questioning to:

    (a)   identify the patterns of behaviour that have developed around the conflicts.
    (b)   formulate ideas on how this pattern maintains important relationships and beliefs in their place of work.
    (c)   explore which behaviours of the interviewee maintain this pattern.

5.   After 10 minutes, the interviewer and observer make a hypothesis.

6.   After 10 minutes, the interviewer questions to explore the hypothesis.

7.   After 10 minutes, the interviewer and observer meet to prepare an intervention.

8.   The interviewer gives the intervention to the interviewee and lets the interviewee give some feedback.

9.   The threesomes are then asked to discuss the process and to particularly address the question of what difference the consultation made to their thinking, or 'What is the problem now?'

Discussion

This is one of the 'classic' exercises we have used for many years. It seems to have the effect of enabling the therapist to see him/herself as a part of a wider system which in turn affects his/her view about a particular family therapy case. We find that this taps a rich vein of systemic thinking which the therapist applies to his therapeutic relationship with the family.

The interviewer and observer gain equally from having to do a real, 'live' consultation. They are galvanized by having to make a real intervention and their learning is enhanced by the feedback they receive from this process.

Exercise 11

1.   The participants are asked to join in foursomes in which one pair forms a client system and creates a script from a real case, but then role-plays the script in an *'ad hoc'* fashion. The other pair forms a worker system, therapist and observer, and works out their contract for working together.

2.   The therapist interviews the clients for about 10 minutes to discuss the problem, map the system of relationships around the problem and try to answer the question of how the problem maintains the balance of beliefs and relationships in the system (the observer may keep time).

3.   The therapist and observer make a hypothesis.

4.   The therapist continues interviewing to explore the hypothesis for another 10 minutes.

     During this period, the observer is asked to observe the system created by the therapist and clients and to interrupt every minute with process comments only, no questions. These should be comments about the process of the family interaction or the family–therapist interaction, to enable the therapist to be attentive to the process while interviewing.

5.   The exercise can be repeated, with the client roles swapping with the therapist and observer roles, asking beforehand of each person, 'What do you want to learn from this exercise second time around?'

6.   This exercise can be discussed in foursomes or the whole group and we have posed the following questions for people to consider. For the therapist: 'How would future work with the family go as a result of this exercise?' For the observer: 'What was the process by which you were able to make comments?'

Discussion
We place great importance on teaching therapists to see the context of their interviews as a process which connects various ideas and

relationships in the family, e.g., 'What does it mean?' or 'How are people organizing relationships?' while they discuss who empties the rubbish. This exercise is very effective in establishing this level of awareness in the therapist's mind.

(E) 'CIRCULAR QUESTIONING' EXERCISES

Exercise 12

1. We preface this exercise by saying it is a chance to play with the questioning and shouldn't be taken too seriously. Then the participants join in pairs, one to be the interviewer and the other the interviewee. The interviewee chooses a relatively neutral topic they would like to be interviewed about – for example, weather, food, travel.

2. Using circular questioning and feedback, the interviewer is asked to try to:

    (a) establish the relationship between the person's beliefs and behaviour on the topic.

    (b) establish the effect these beliefs and behaviour have on two or three relationships in the person's life.

3. After about 10 minutes, there is a break and the interviewer is asked to imagine that beliefs and behaviour are likely to be changing over time and what might be the effect of these changes on relationships. We ask them to continue interviewing for another 5 to 10 minutes without letting the other know what their hypothesis is.

4. The interviewer then shares his/her hypothesis and asks for comments from the interviewee. The interviewee comments on whether anything surprising has emerged so far.

5. This is usefully discussed in the whole group.

Discussion
This is another of the 'classic' exercises which introduces the experience of circular questioning in a context which is playful and less stressful than a clinical setting. We always precede this exercise with some discussion about the need to listen carefully to each reply and base the next question on the previous reply. Also, we emphasize the need to very slowly widen the system by making linking or connecting questions from each reply.

Exercise 13

1.   The participants are asked to join in threesomes, an inter-
      viewer, interviewee and observer. The interviewee agrees
      to be interviewed about the weather, food, or other topic
      he/she chooses.

2.   The interviewer asks circular questions to map the signif-
      icant system around the interviewee's views on the subject
      chosen.

      The observer looks at ways the interviewee organizes the
      interviewer and also offers help in the form of verbatim
      questions of a sequential nature following the feedback
      (this exercise can be modified for use with two people by
      leaving out the observer).

3.   After 10 minutes, the interviewer and observer make a
      hypothesis about possible difficulties based on information
      gathered so far.

4.   After 10 minutes, the interviewer asks more questions
      exploring their hypothesis.

5.   After 10 minutes, the interviewer and observer make an
      intervention, taking 5 minutes. All the interviewees join in
      a group together to discuss issues raised by the experience
      of being interviewed.

6.   After 10 minutes, the interviewer makes an intervention.

7.   The whole group can then discuss the exercise with inter-
      viewees giving feedback on the effect of the intervention on
      their views.

      This exercise can be varied or added to by the interviewee
      presenting a case he/she is working with or by the inter-
      viewee discussing the place of family therapy in his/her
      agency.

Discussion

By introducing an observer to this exercise, we facilitate the interviewer to think at two levels: the level of engaging the interviewee and listening to content; and the level of seeing the interview as a larger process which includes the interviewer as part of the system. Also when the observer offers comments or questions, the therapist is freed to move his/her thinking on to new areas, and has an experience of getting 'unstuck'.

(F) 'TEAM MIND' EXERCISES

Exercise 14 – The *'ad hoc'* family system

We have frequently used the exercise, first presented to us by Boscolo and Cecchin, of interviewing an *'ad hoc'* family. In such an exercise, a group of three or four people are asked to form themselves into some sort of system without any script or opportunity to discuss their notes. This can be a family or any working group. We usually give instructions such as, "We would like you to become a group which is interconnected in some way and has a problem requiring a consultation." We ask the group not to discuss anything together but simply to respond to the feedback created during the interview. Then the therapist begins the process by asking the group to introduce themselves, describe their relationships to each other or state their problem. Once one person responds to the first question, the system begins to take shape and, as each member of the group continues to respond to the previous comments, an *'ad hoc'* system very quickly takes a shape of its own.

A great advantage of this exercise is that both participants and observers have a vivid experience of the way systems are formed in relation to the feedback process created by a therapist; and that they are not dependent on past history or agreed belief systems in order to have a coherent pattern of behaviour.

One example of an *'ad hoc'* family exercise which we have used is:

1.   Four participants are asked to become an *'ad hoc'* family which is interviewed by one of the course leaders.

2.   The other participants are asked to get into groups and discuss during several breaks in the interview how they see this group becoming a system.

3.   We have also asked one member of these groups to highlight a particular answer given by the family to one of the interviewer's questions, as an example of an answer given and the next member would comment on this comment and so on until the systemic view emerged (see Exercise 16 – The Sequential Discussion).

Discussion

The 'ad hoc' family exercise lends itself to many variations which can be designed to suit the particular needs of the group. However, we have found that when groups are interviewed with no script whatsoever, it makes a powerful impact on the participants.

Exercise 15

1. In a group of 8, one person briefly presents a case they are working with. Each person asks one question in turn, going around the circle in sequence, using the previous answer to create a question.

2. The seven questioners join in smaller groupings of two or three to make a hypothesis about the case and then ask more questions as before to explore the hypothesis.

3. During this round of questions, we ask that each question should be followed by one or two others which are based directly on the feedback.

Discussion
The importance of building a cumulative picture of the family is emphasized in this exercise. Each participant has to choose a question which makes sense in the context of all the questions which have preceded it. Questions therefore become economical and penetrating. The presenter is pushed toward a systemic view of the case by different questions which reflect different hypotheses, but may also find the questioning confusing. This should be addressed. Finally, we find that this is an efficient way to generate new hypotheses for stuck cases.

Exercise 16 – 'The sequential discussion'

1. When a small group of three or four are observing clinical material or videotape or listening to a verbal presentation of a case, we ask one member of the group to begin by making a brief comment about what they think or observe in the material. The next person in the circle comments on the first comment and then adds a brief observation of their own. The third does the same and so on, in sequence, around the circle. This sequential process is usually followed for 5 or 6 'rounds' (or 5–10 minutes).

2. Following this, the group is then asked to continue the sequential discussion to arrive at a statement or formulation of the case which best represents a shared or consensual reality.

3. At the end of the exercise, it is often illuminating for the group members to share their experience of the process of participating in such a discussion.

Discussion

We use this type of discussion very frequently. It not only 'levels' all the participants, allowing everyone an equal say, but most importantly, they experience for themselves the creation of a systemic reality. Their own views are modified and shaped by others, and, when successful, the final formulation is an example of a reality which is created through a process and is larger than the sum of the individual members.

(G) 'OBSERVATION OF OWN LEARNING PROCESS' EXERCISES

Exercise 17

1.   The participants are asked to join in threesomes and choose to be interviewer, interviewee and observer. The interviewer is asked to pose the following questions.

    (a)   Who is the least interested in the systemic ideas you may bring back from the course?

    (b)   What is your explanation for this lack of interest?

    (c)   How does this lack of interest organize your relationship with this person?

    (d)   What problems would be created for the agency if this person became interested in systemic thinking?

    (e)   What would you need from this course to reassure the least interested/most interested person in the agency that it would not be under threat from these ideas?

2.   The interviewer and observer then discuss the answers and make two interventions:

    (a)   What this person needs to do to reassure the person who is least interested that things might not change too much.

    (b)   What this person needs to do to introduce some ideas that could challenge the system.

The interviewees join together in a group and make an intervention to the course.

3.   The interviewers then deliver the interventions to the interviewees and the interviewees give feedback about the effect of the interventions.

4.   In the whole group, the exercise is discussed and interviewees give the intervention to the course.

5.   The whole group is invited to guess at the hypothesis that generated the questions used in the interviewing.

Discussion

This exercise, coming near the beginning of a course, explores the participants' own 'ecology of ideas'. We assume that each person will want to develop some new ideas and preserve some old ones and that this relationship has to be explored, through such an exercise, to enable the learning process to begin. The ecology of the individual is linked to the ecology of the agency. Also, by asking participants to make an intervention to the course, we find, they become more engaged in the learning which occurs through the large group process.

Exercise 18

1.   The participants are asked to join in foursomes to discuss what specific things make it difficult for them to develop themselves further as family therapists in their own agencies.

2.   In each foursome, two people are asked to form an interviewing team to interview one person. The fourth person joins the interviewers as an observer.

3.   The interviewers are asked to try to identify the pattern of behaviour and relationships that have developed around the attempt and the obstacles to developing as a family therapist in the agency.

4.   They are also asked to try to identify how this pattern maintains important relationships or beliefs in the agency. The interviewee thinks about what he or she does to maintain the problem.

5.   The interviewing team then makes an intervention based on their understanding of the system and the interviewee gives feedback on its effect.

6.   The whole group discusses the exercise. They may be asked to think about the question, "What is the problem now?"

Discussion
This exercise combines some of our thinking about the agency ecology (described above) with a more fully developed agency consultation. Here, we stress the connection between the individual and the pattern observed within the agency. This places the interviewee squarely in the system he/she is observing and thereby offers a new systemic perspective of the agency and its 'problems'.

Exercise 19

1.   Near the beginning of a course, participants are asked to join in threesomes with an interviewer, observer and interviewee. The interviewer is to find out for the interviewee how coming on the course will affect significant relationships in the working context if his/her expectations of the course are met. This takes 10 minutes.

2.   The observer is asked to develop ideas about the system emerging between the interviewer and the interviewee.

3.   Following the interview, each is asked to consider a particular question:

   (a)   *To the observer:* "How would you describe the interviewer and interviewee as an emerging system? How did the feedback between one and the other create this?"

   (b)   *To the interviewee:* "In what ways did the exercise affect your thinking about your agency and the learning you are expecting on the course?"

   (c)   *To the interviewer:* "What information organized you in trying to find out about the interviewee's network of relationships and learning?"

4.   The whole group may then discuss the themes emerging from the exercise.

5.   The exercise can be repeated with the participants swapping roles as follows. The interviewer becomes the observer, the observer becomes the interviewee, and the interviewee becomes the interviewer. After about 5 minutes of this second round, the groups are stopped and the interviewer and observer are asked to briefly make a hypothesis. Then they continue the interview focusing on their hypothesis for another 5 minutes.

6.   After the interview, each is asked to consider the following question:

(a)   *To the observer:* "What effect did having been an interviewer have on you as an observer this time?"

(b)   *To the interviewee:* "How was the interview different after the hypothesis-making?"

(c)   *To the interviewer:* "What did you learn about interviewing?"

Discussion
This is a very complex and powerful exercise. It is based on the premise that the participants' expectations are linked to their position in their agencies, but many aspects of systemic thinking are explored along the way. Each participant is asked to observe an unfolding system, to develop an interview with a hypothesis and to observe himself/herself in his/her own learning process.

Exercise 20
The participants are asked to join in foursomes to discuss the link between their own beliefs and their agency beliefs, answering the following questions:

(a)   In what ways do your beliefs (or your personal epistemology) conflict with that of your agency? How does it show?

(b)   What important factors organize your relationships with your clients and with your agency?

(c)   How does this affect your work?

(d)   Is any colleague aware of these conflicts and how?

(e)   What will happen to these conflicts?

(f)   What would be the effect of changes in your beliefs or personal epistemology on your work in your agency?

Discussion
This exercise places its emphasis on the belief system of the individual and agency and then connects it to the relationships.

Exercise 21

1.   The participants are asked to join in pairs, each person to interview the other about:

(a)   The ideas and skills each wants to put into practice from the course in his/her agency.

(b)   What would be the effect on relationships with colleagues and clients – naming these and defining the changes.

2.   The interviewer then makes a hypothesis about what is under threat if change occurs.

3.   The interviewer continues to ask more questions, following the feedback.

4.   The interviewer stops to make an intervention. The interviewee gives feedback when it has been given.

5.   The whole group may discuss what people are to do with the new information from the course in relation to their agencies.

Discussion
Here, the beliefs and relationships are linked more closely. These two exercises accomplish similar aims but we might prefer one because the emphasis suits us or the group as we are developing on a course at that time.

Exercise 22
This is a brief exercise for the end of the course. The participants
are asked to join in threesomes and make a hypothesis about
how the teachers could end the course in a way which would
make it possible for them to carry on with their learning.

Discussion
*We like to draw people's attention to the fact that they are learning
through the structure of the course and invite them to create a context
for their own learning by designing part of the course to suit their
needs. Participants 'learn about learning' by designing exercises for
each other, and it is particularly helpful for those who will be teaching
in other settings.*

(H) 'CASE DISCUSSION' EXERCISES

Exercise 23 – The reflecting team discussion

Participants learn a great deal from presenting their own cases and listening to the views of other people. However, we often find that a direct discussion of a case fails to shift the basic premises which the presenter brings to the case. This exercise breaks the traditional pattern of reciprocal discussion between presenter and listener by forbidding discussion and moving the presenter to an observer position. It also distances the presenter from his own premises by treating his views as information about the presenter's system.

1.   Participants are asked to get into groups of three, four or five. One person is asked to present a case he or she is feeling stuck with and to say something about the therapy, why he/she feels stuck, and what he/she has done to get 'unstuck'. This should not go on for longer than 10 minutes.

2.   The others in the group then discuss the case together, but not with the presenter, who becomes an observer, forbidden to speak or even correct any misunderstanding. The group should arrive at some systemic understanding of why this person is stuck with this case. This should take about 10 minutes. We often ask the group to speak in the sequential way described earlier (Exercise 16).

3.   The presenter is then invited to comment on the discussion. He or she usually has views about what seemed accurate or inaccurate, helpful or unhelpful. This should last only a few minutes. The presenter should be asked to refrain from trying to explain his views, and merely invited to comment on the discussion.

4.   Again the group turn to each other to discuss the comments made by the presenter. These comments should be discussed as information to enable the group to develop further their systemic formulation about the case. They can ask themselves, "What does it tell us about this system, that the presenter has chosen to comment on these partic-

ular aspects of our discussion?" This takes about 5 minutes.

5.   The presenter can be invited to comment on this *second* discussion and the group can again discuss the presenter's comments.

The experience usually takes about 30 minutes. A variation which we have used successfully is to designate two of the group to be an observing group, who observe the interaction between the presenter and the group and end the exercise with their final comments.

(I) ON GETTING STUCK

Exercise 24

During one workshop, we felt we had not engaged the group in creating an interesting learning context with us. During a break, we discussed this, pondered, and made a hypothesis that some of the participants weren't very keen to learn new ideas because they were connected to agencies which maintained this view of learning and of the workshop. We decided to do an exercise which would explore this hypothesis.

We asked the participants to get into pairs and interview each other to explore the questions:

(a) Who in your agency is least interested in your being on this workshop?

(b) What is your explanation for this lack of interest?

(c) In what way does this lack of interest maintain their relationship with this person?

(d) What problems would be created for the agency if this person were to become interested in systemic thinking?

(e) What would you need from this course to reassure the least interested people in the agency?

Discussion
The exercise had the powerful effect of engaging the group members and freeing us from feeling we had to overcome any lack of interest. We continued teaching as though we could step down a gear and as a result, the others became more interested in what we were teaching.

(J) EXERCISES ARISING FROM CONSULTATION

We tend to treat requests for consultation rather like a referral letter about a family. Following the request, we would make a hypothesis about what the agency wants. People think they know what they want but we would try to develop ideas to answer their request in a way that is unpredictable, so as to begin making new connections and to broaden the context in which they make the request. The aim would be to create a space in which they feel safe and free to work, rather than specifically delivering the goods they have asked for.

An example of this kind of request was the one from a school in which they asked us to offer a consultation to the staff group to improve communication and co-operation amongst the group members. We met with the headmaster to discuss the background to the problem and we made hypotheses about the way the problem led to the group feeling stuck, and the wider meaning which 'being stuck' might have within the school system. Based on our hypothesis, we decided that our invitation to provide a consultation was seen as one aspect of the failed attempt to solve the problem and therefore we could not offer a consultation which was seen as a consultation. Therefore, we decided to design an exercise which would address problems within the system in such a way that we did not appear to be giving a consultation to the group process.

1. The teaching staff group was arranged in four groups of eight people. Each member was asked to play a particular role. These were:

    (a) A member of the school board plus his/her observer;

    (b) The headmaster of the school plus his/her observer;

    (c) A classroom teacher plus his/her observer;

    (d) A parent plus his/her observer;

2. Each member of the group was given a script, which were as follows:

(a) *For the member of the school board:*
     "The board has no choice but to make significant cuts in the budget, but has to find a way to do this that maintains the loyalty of staff and parents to the school."

(b) *For the headmaster:*
     "The head wants to protect his staff and fight the cuts, but knows that if he is not co-operative his school will be penalized."

(c) *For the classroom teacher:*
     "You have well-developed ideas about the ways your own teaching can be effective and maintain standards; you see the proposed cuts as forcing you to compromise and lower your standards."

(d) *For the parent:*
     "You feel that at a time of dwindling resources, higher academic standards are required to ensure no child misses out on its future."

Each of the groups was given the main script, which read:
"The school will have to make budget cuts, but everyone involved wants to do so without lowering the standards of the school."

Each of the group members was given the following instruction which they discussed with their observer:
"Using your script as a starting point, let yourself get involved in a discussion but maintain your position."

The observer was asked to watch the way his/her partner was affected by what the other people said.

3.   After 10 minutes, they were asked to have a break and each member was asked to share their impressions with their own observer only and to discuss the losses and gains each of the other three role-playing members would face if he or she were to change his/her position.

4.   On the basis of this discussion, each role-playing member

was asked to take a different line of argument to allow the others to accommodate to a new position. This break took about 15 minutes.

5.   The group were then asked to have a second discussion period of 10 minutes.

6.   We then combined small groups to make groups of 16 in order to discuss what their experiences were. The groups were interviewed by one of the consultants. This took about 15 minutes.

7.   We then asked the groups to go back to their original groups of 8 for a final discussion and we said that we were going to set each group a task, which was to discuss, "What do you think we (the consultants) have seen and learned about the difficulties of negotiating change in a school system?" Then, after about 10 minutes, we interrupted the groups and asked them to consider the question, "What other things should we understand which have not emerged in the discussion so far?" This was discussed for another 10 minutes.

8.   We ended the consultation by sharing our own formulation of the system and discussing it with the large group.

Discussion
We find that using scripts allows participants to get close to the issues that concern them, while allowing them the safety of being in a role. They can 'play' with new ideas and new ways of behaving in a situation which resembles the problem-based context. We found that this exercise cooled down a heated atmosphere and allowed participants to listen to each other and explore new relationships in a safe environment.

Following the consultation, we heard from the headmaster a few weeks later that the atmosphere in the staff group had changed and that they had decided to alter the structure of their staff meetings by organizing themselves into small discussion groups, consisting of teachers with different roles. These groups discussed particular topics and then fed them back to the large group.

Conclusions

We said at the beginning of this book that we hoped readers would use it as a resource. It is, of course, *not* the definitive text on teaching systemic thinking; writing it has been an intervention in our own thinking.

We began with a desire to share some the ideas we have found helpful in our own teaching of systemic thinking in various settings. To do this, we referred to the questions that trainees and workshop participants have asked us. These questions range widely (as you now know, having read thus far in the text) over the content and the method – the 'what' and the 'how' – of our teaching.

Writing this booklet has highlighted our own process in attempting to respond in a useful way to trainees' requests. We invariably put their requests and questions into the context of the trainees' own learning. We also put them into a context: the potential effect on relationships in the trainees' professional (and sometimes personal) networks that any successful learning of a particular aspect of systemic thinking or practice could bring about.

Hypothesizing about the meaning of the changes that could come about as a result of learning something makes it easier for us as teachers to design exercises, devise tasks and answer questions. These must be constructed in a way that takes into account not only the trainees' wishes to acquire more knowledge, expertise and the chance to practice (which of course are valid requests in their own right); but also the way in which wanting this kind of change often presents a dilemma for trainees, who in the same way as family members (who want to see things change) find themselves threatening the balance between stability and change in their system.

Our approach to teaching systemic thinking aims to help trainees to experience the way in which learning occurs. When trainees acknowledge how the wish for more knowledge is part of the constant oscillation between the wish for stability and the wish for change in their ecology of ideas, then they can explore how this wish may affect their networks of relationships.

We hope and expect that readers who have to teach will develop their own processes for discovering the meaning of a request for teaching input and develop new and creative ways to respond to the requests they receive.

The next question we ask when teaching is: "What will trainees and workshop participants be doing in a few months or a year's time, that will stimulate our own thinking and curiosity?"

Writing and thinking about teaching systemic thinking has made us as teachers more aware of the importance of communicating, and that teaching is a process of sharing what we understand at time 'A' and having our thinking and work enriched in time 'B' by the ways in which trainees interact with us and our ideas.

Ensuring that readers appreciate the need to be open to feedback in whichever system they work or teach (because we think this is the most effective way of demonstrating and developing systemic thinking) is a major theme that has emerged in writing this book. To continue to teach well, we must see ourselves as part of the teaching/learning system, and also see ourselves as not able *not to be affected ourselves* by the teaching/learning process.

References

Andersen, T. (1984) 'Consultation: would you like co-evolution instead of referral?' *Family Systems Medicine*, 2, 4.

Andersen, T. (1987) 'The reflecting team: dialogue and meta-dialogue in clinical work.' (Unpublished Manuscript).

Anderson, H., Goolishian, H. and Windermand, L. (1987) 'Problem determined systems: towards transformation in family therapy.' *Journal of Strategic and Systemic Therapies*, 5, 4, pp. 1–13.

Bateson, G. (1973) 'The cybernetics of "self": a theory of alcoholism,' in *Steps to an Ecology of Mind*. London: Paladin, pp. 280–308.

Bateson, G. (1973) 'The logical categories of learning and communication,' in *Steps to an Ecology of Mind*. London: Paladin, pp. 250–279.

Bennun, I. (1986) 'Evaluating family therapy: a comparison of the Milan and problem solving approaches.' *Journal of Family Therapy*, 8, 3, pp. 235–242.

Blount, A. (1985) 'Towards a "systemically" organized mental health centre.' In Campbell, D. and Draper, R. (Eds.), *Applications of Systemic Family Therapy: the Milan Approach*. London: Grune and Stratton.

Boscolo, L. and Cecchin, G. (1982) 'Training in systemic therapy at the Milan Centre.' In Whiffen, R. and Byng-Hall, J. (Eds.), *Family Therapy Supervision: Recent Developments in Practice.* London: Academic Press.

Boscolo, L., Cecchin, G., Campbell, D. and Draper, R. (1985) 'Twenty more questions – selections from a discussion between the Milan Associates and the Editors.' In Campbell, D. and Draper, R. (Eds.), *Applications of Systemic Family Therapy: the Milan Approach.* London: Grune and Stratton.

Campbell, D. (1985) 'The consultation interview.' In Campbell, D. and Draper, R. (Eds.), *Applications of Systemic Family Therapy: the Milan Approach.* London: Grune and Stratton.

Campbell, D. and Draper, R. (Eds.), (1985) *Applications of Systemic Family Therapy: the Milan Approach.* London: Grune and Stratton.

Campbell, D., Reder, P., Draper, R. and Pollard, D. (1983) *Working with the Milan Method: Twenty Questions.* Occasional Paper, London: Institute of Family Therapy.

Castellucci, A., Fruggeri, L. and Marzari, M. (1985) 'Instability and evolutionary change in a psychiatric community.' In Campbell, D. and Draper, R. (Eds.), *Applications of Systemic Family Therapy: the Milan Approach.* London: Grune and Stratton.

Cecchin G. and Fruggeri, L. (1986) 'Consultation with mental health system teams in Italy.' In Wynne, L., McDaniel, S. and Weber, G. (Eds.), *Systems Consultation: New Perspectives for Family Therapy.* New York: Guilford Press.

Cronen, V., Johnson, K. and Lannamann, J. (1982) 'Paradoxes, double binds and reflexive loops: an alternative theoretical perspective.' *Family Process,* **20**, pp. 91–112.

Cronen, V. and Pearce, B. (1985) 'Towards an explanation of how the Milan method works: an invitation to a systemic epistemology and the evolution of family systems.' In Campbell, D. and Draper, R. (Eds.), *Applications of Systemic Family Therapy: the Milan Approach.* London: Grune and Stratton.

Cronen, V., Pearce, B. and Tomm, K. (1985) 'A dialectic view of personal change.' In Gergen, K. and Davis, K. (Eds.), *The Social Construction of the Person.* New York: Springer Verlag.

Dell, P.F. (1982) 'Beyond homeostasis: toward a concept of coherence.' *Family Process,* **21**, pp. 21–42.

Dell, P.F. (1985) 'Understanding Bateson and Maturana: towards a biological foundation for the social sciences.' *Journal of Marital and Family Therapy*, **11**, pp. 1–20.

Dell, P.F. (1984) 'Why family therapy should go beyond homeostasis: a Kuhnian reply to Ariel, Carel and Tyano.' *Journal of Marital and Family Therapy*, **10**, 4, pp. 351–356.

Fruggeri, L., Dotti, D., Ferrari, R. and Matteini, M. (1985) 'The systemic approach in a mental health service.' In Campbell, D. and Draper, R. (Eds.), *Applications of Systemic Family Therapy: the Milan Approach*. London: Grune and Stratton.

Hoffman, L. (1985) 'Beyond power and control: toward a "second order" family systems therapy.' *Family Systems Medicine*, **3**, 4, pp. 381–396.

Hoffman, L. (1981) *Foundations of Family Therapy*. New York: Basic Books.

Keeney, B. (1983) *Aesthetics of Change*. New York: Guilford Press.

Keeney, B. and Sprenkle, D. (1982) 'Ecosystemic epistemology: critical implications of the aesthetics and pragmatics of family therapy.' *Family Process*, **21**, 1, pp. 1–19.

Lane, G. and Russell, T. (1987) 'Neutrality versus social control.' *Family Therapy Networker*, May–June, pp. 52–56.

Levin, S., Raser, J., Niles, C. and Reese, A. (1987) 'Beyond family systems – Forward problem systems: some clinical implications.' *Journal of Strategic and Systemic Therapies*, 5, 4, pp. 62–69.

MacKinnon, L., Parry, A. and Black, R. (1984) 'Strategies of family therapy: the relationship to styles of family functioning.' *Journal of Strategic and Systemic Therapies*, **3**, 3, pp. 6–22.

Maturana, H. (1978) 'Biology of language: the epistemology of reality.' In Miller, G.A. and Lennenberg, E. (Eds.), *Psychology and Biology of Language and Thought*. New York: Academic Press.

Maturana, H. and Varela, F. (1980) *Autopoiesis and Cognition: the Realization of the Living*. Reidel, Holland.

Mendez, C.L., Coddou, F. and Maturana, H. (1988) 'The bringing forth of pathology.' *Irish Journal of Psychology*, Special issue: Constructivism.

Penn, P. (1982) 'Circular questioning.' *Family Process*, **21**, 3, pp. 267–280.

Penn, P. (1985) 'Feed-forward: future questions, future maps.' *Family Process*, **24**, 3, pp. 299–310.

Pirrotta, S. (1984) 'Milan revisited: a comparison of the two Milan schools.' *Journal of Strategic and Systemic Therapies*, **3**, 4, pp. 3–15.

Prigogine, I. and Stengers, I. (1977) 'New alliance, 2. Extended dynamics – towards a human science of nature.' *Scientia*, **112**, pp. 617–653.

Ricci, C. and Selvini Palazzoli, M. (1984) 'Interactional complexity and communication.' *Family Process*, **23**, pp. 169–176.

Selvini Palazzoli, M. (1974) *Self Starvation*. London: Human Context Books.

Selvini Palazzoli, M., Boscolo, L., Cecchin, G. and Prata, G. (1977) 'Family rituals: a powerful tool in family therapy.' *Family Process*, **16**, 4, pp. 169–176.

Selvini Palazzoli, M., Boscolo, L., Cecchin, G. and Prata, G. (1978) *Paradox and Counterparadox*. New York: Aronson.

Selvini Palazzoli, M., Boscolo, L., Cecchin, G. and Prata, G. (1978) 'A ritualized prescription in family therapy: odd days and even days.' *Journal of Marriage and Family Counselling*, pp. 3–8.

Selvini Palazzoli, M., Boscolo, L., Cecchin, G. and Prata, G. (1980) 'The problem of the referring person.' *Journal of Marital and Family Therapy*, **6**, 1, pp. 3–9.

Selvini Palazzoli, M., Boscolo, L., Cecchin, G. and Prata, G. (1980) 'Hypothesizing – circularity – neutrality: three guidelines for the conductor of the session.' *Family Process*, **19**, 1, pp. 3–12.

Selvini Palazzoli, M. and Prata, G. (1983) 'A new method for therapy and research in the treatment of schizophrenic families.' In Stierlin, H., Wynne, L.C. and Wirsching, M. (Eds.), *Psychosocial Intervention in Schizophrenia: an International View*. Berlin: Springer.

Selvini Palazzoli, M. (1983) 'The emergence of a comprehensive systems approach.' *Journal of Family Therapy*, **5**, pp. 165–177.

Selvini Palazzoli, M. (1984) 'Behind the scenes of the organization: some guidelines for the expert in human relations.' *Journal of Family Therapy*, **6**, pp. 299–307.

Selvini Palazzoli, M. (1985) 'The emergence of a comprehensive systems approach: supervisor and team problems in a district psychiatric centre.' *Journal of Family Therapy*, **7**, pp. 135–146.

Selvini Palazzoli, M. (1985) 'The problem of the sibling as the referring person.' *Journal of Marital and Family Therapy*, **11**, 1, pp. 21–34.

Selvini Palazzoli, M. (1986) 'Towards a general model of psychotic family games.' *Journal of Marital and Family Therapy*, **12**, 4, pp. 339–349.

Selvini Palazzoli, M. and Viaro, M. (1988) 'The anorectic process in the family: a six-stage model as a guide for individual therapy.' *Family Process*, **27**, pp. 129–148.

Speed, B. (1985) 'Evaluating the Milan approach.' In Campbell, D. and Draper, R. (Eds.), *Applications of Systemic Family Therapy: the Milan Approach*. London: Grune and Stratton.

Tomm, K. (1985) 'Circular interviewing: a multifaceted clinical tool.' In Campbell, D. and Draper, R. (Eds.), *Applications of Systemic Family Therapy: the Milan Approach*. London: Grune and Stratton.

Tomm, K. (1987) 'Interventive interviewing: Part I. Strategizing as a fourth guideline for the therapist.' *Family Process*, **26**, pp. 3–13.

Tomm, K. (1987) 'Interventive interviewing: Part II. Reflexive questioning as a means to enable self healing.' *Family Process*, **26**, pp. 167–183.

Tomm, K. (1984) 'One perspective on the Milan systemic approach: Part I. Overview of development, theory and practice.' *Journal of Marital and Family Therapy*, **10**, 2, pp. 113–125.

Tomm, K. (1984) 'One perspective on the Milan systemic approach: Part II. Description of session format, interviewing style and interventions.' *Journal of Marital and Family Therapy*, **10**, 3, pp. 253–271.

Tomm, K. and Wright, L. (1982) 'Multilevel training and supervision in an outpatient service programme.' In Whiffen, R. and Byng-Hall, J. (Eds.), *Family Therapy Supervision: Recent Developments in Practice*. London: Academic Press.

Ugazio, V. (1985) 'Hypothesis making: the Milan approach

revisited.' In Campbell, D. and Draper, R. (Eds.), *Applications of Systemic Family Therapy: the Milan Approach*. London: Grune and Stratton.

Van Trommel, M. (1984) 'A consultation method addressing the therapist–family system.' *Family Process*, 23, 4, pp. 469–480.

Varela, F. (1979) *Principles of Biological Autonomy*. New York: North Holland Press.

Viaro, M. and Leonardo, P. (1982) 'Getting and giving information: analysis of a particular interview strategy.' *Family Process*, 22, pp. 27–42.

Viaro, M. and Leonardo, P. (1986) 'The evolution of the interview technique: a comparison between former and present strategy.' *Journal of Strategic and Systemic Therapies*, 5, 1 & 2, pp. 14–30.

Von Glasersfeld, E. (1984) 'An introduction to radical constructivism.' In Watzlawick, P. (Ed.), *The Invented Reality*. New York: W.W. Norton.

Watzlawick, P., Beavin, J. and Jackson, D. (1967) *Pragmatics of Human Communication*. New York: W.W. Norton.

Watzlawick, P., Weakland, J.H. and Fisch, R. (1974) *Change: Principles of Problem Formation and Problem Resolution*. New York: W.W. Norton.